Not of This Worldview

Poetry for the Kingdom Among Us

— RICHARD S. BRIGGS —

Sacristy Press
PO Box 612, Durham, DH1 9HT

www.sacristy.co.uk

First published in 2021 by Sacristy Press, Durham.

Sacristy Limited, registered in England & Wales, number 7565667

British Library Cataloguing-in-Publication Data
A catalogue record for the book is available from the British Library

ISBN 978-1-78959-158-3

To Patricia

lifelong friend

Contents

Prelude

In my day job ... I am privileged to work for God's kingdom. I am a teacher, a preacher, a lecturer, a minister, a tutor, a mentor, and—most of all—a servant of the Word in response to whom all our words are offered. All along the way, whether at home or abroad, I have loved the moments when the kingdom of God breaks through into our everyday world, and casts strange light on daily life. It is those moments I seek to capture here: moments when we are reminded that the view of the disciple is not the view of the world in which we live; that the kingdom for which we reach is not of this worldview.

A poet is a testimony of sorts to the oddness of God in a society that pretends to be all efficiency and effect. Poetic words trip and stumble slowly. I have written these poems over at least thirty years, on and off. Only a very few of them have been published before, and none of them in precisely the form they take here. In the end, dwelling in England's glorious North East, and working in the shadow of Durham Cathedral, the mysteries of this wonderful place seemed to call forth these words. Finally comes the poet, as Walt Whitman once said—though he went on to describe the poet as "the true son of God" (in *Leaves of Grass*). Another Walter (Brueggemann) then adopted the phrase to describe the sages of the Old Testament. And here I join at the end of that long line.

So welcome. See differently. Tread carefully. In the words of Jesus in the Gospel according to St Luke, we will not say "Here it is!" or "There it is!", but even so, the kingdom will be among us (Luke 17:21).

If we have eyes to see.

Richard Briggs
Feast of James the Apostle
July 2020

A Prayer

Lord give us eyes to see

And ears to hear

Open hearts

And open minds

Beyond, between, behind the veil

This theatre—this playground—this warzone

This staging of a glory beyond our wisest dreams

This reshuffled reality

With its character notes always in place, ringing, resilient:

    Always hoping

    Always longing

    Always rewarding

    Always yours.

Amen.

The Gift of Eyes to See

The hearing ear and the seeing eye—the
LORD has made them both.

Proverbs 20:12

The gift of eyes to see is a very strange gift
Wrapped in flesh and bones, encased in mystery
Encased in flesh and blood, wired to the brain
A very strange gift is the gift of eyes to see

The hearing pair of ears is another graced gift
Turning to and fro, learning as it hears
Ranging near and far, sounding to the soul
Another graced gift is the hearing pair of ears

The heart that attends is a world-shaping gift
Beating out grace for enemies and friends
Working out love, mind and soul and strength
A world-shaping gift is the heart that attends

The life we are given is embodied as gift
Dwelling in us—by the Spirit driven
Brimming with life—eyes and ears and heart
Embodied as gift is the life we are given

The Father of lights is the giver of gifts
May our eyes learn to discern the sights
Every good gift comes down from above
The giver of gifts is the Father of lights

Durham Cathedral

Cart stopped in mud
Riverrun, past the castle keep
We build it here
Tomb of St Cuthbert

Eyes stopped in awe
Heartrun, wait with baited breath
We worship here
Rock of the ages

Time stopped in love
Spiritrun, gift of lifted light
We live it here
Shape of a Sabbath

Souls stopped in calm
Worshiprun, fly in rising song
We pray it here
Word of the heavens

God stopped in us
Joyrun, run to wonders new
We sense it here
Hope of the future

The Village Church of St Mary the Virgin, Sherburn

No form or majesty that we should marvel at it
Nothing in its appearance that we should desire it

Bricks and mortar
Damp carpets and noisy heaters
But here it is that God has borne our infirmities
    and carried our diseases.

Pews and hymn books
Sunday school paintings
And here it is that God has met us in our needs
    and in each other.

Christmas decorations
Remembrance Day parades
As here it is that God walks with us in rhythms of the year.

Churchyard graves
Stained glass windows
For here it is that God comforts us in our
    grief and raises us to new life.

Bread and wine.
Word and song.
Here it is that God delights to be with us
In and with and through our joy and fear.

A church not made with hands
Inside a church of wood and stone—
Our God is on the move,
And rooted here.

Conversion Takes Its Time

The fork upon the road is barely sought
I took the road less travelled in my joy
I found the way was harder than I thought

With zeal I set out thinking myself taught
In truth I was no different from a boy
The fork upon the road is barely sought

The seed that fell on rock had never caught
The thorns that sprang up started to annoy
I found the way was harder than I thought

The gift of life is never truly bought
The failures of my faith have left me coy
The fork upon the road is barely sought

The options close around me, come to naught
I turn again and sweetest songs employ
I found the way was harder than I thought

Thus in and out of season love has brought
A faith that moth and rust shall not destroy
The fork upon the road is barely sought
I found the way was harder than I thought

The Strange New World of Genesis 1

*Not a translation of Genesis 1, but
a celebration of its style*

God begins: it's heaven-and-earth time.

Well the earth was like a wishy-washy mish-mash
And there above the deepest darkest deep
The Spirit-God / the breath of God / the wind of God
Was hushing all the wildness to sleep.

And God said "What we need in here is light"
The light was pretty good, He had to say
He split the light and darkness from each other
And right away He had him night and day.

Pretty good!
What a (night and) day that was
A first day.

A dome was placed amidst the massive waters
To separate the waters from the waters
So that's . . .
A dome and some separated waters
And water everywhere in watery flow
With water up above the dome
And water underneath the dome
—It was wet (and it was good) and it was so.

That dome needs a name.
Let's call it heaven.

What a day that was
Day two.

Now the water under heaven over here
Piles up and lets the solid ground appear
Call these gathered waters earth and seas
Then fill the earth richly
And thus it unwinds:
Sprouting things will sprout,
Herbs and seeding things will seed
Trees with fruit
Will do their fruit
According to their need
And all the things with seeds in
Each according to their kinds.

Pretty good!
What a day that was
Day three.

The lights are like the tabernacle lights
The lights that mark the day out from the night
They mark the signs and seasons and the years
And mark the days they lead on out to birth
They fly across the vast expanse of dome-iness
The big light and the small light giving
   light upon the earth.
Oh and the stars.
The big light and the small light and the stars
Lighting up the dome around the earth.

Pretty good!
What a day that was
Day four.

The swarming things are swarming in the water
The living souls of swarming things are there
The flying things are flying in the water that is sky
And the great sea-monsters underneath are going by
And every living thing,
And now they're swarming in the water
All the winged flying things according to their kinds
All the flying swarmers are turning up for blessing
And fruitfulness and multiplying swarm and fill the sky.

Pretty good!
What a day that was
Day five.

It's filling time.
Living creatures fill the earth, each, kind, and so forth
Living things, creeping things, behemoth, earth-fillers
And here they come: beasting, and

    living, and ground-creeping
And it's pretty good.
Then *Adam*, as the image of God
—causing a pause for underlining—

    As the image of God He made him

    That's male and female, as He created them

    —but enough underlining, as onward we go:
With blessing!
With being fruitful and multiplying and

    filling the earth and subduing it
And dominating the fish
No wait, not just the fish
But the birds in the dome

    and all the creeping things on earth
As much as there is to live and fly and creep and breathe—
With a vegan diet thrown in.
Did we leave anything out?
. . . No, we did not.

That's not just pretty good. It's really pretty very good.
What a day *that* was!
Day six.

Dome and planet finished.

Oh and the stars.

God is finished working, God is sabbathing

Call it the seventh day, call it sabbath.

A blessing,

Holiness,

It is done.

And that's the story of the heavens and the earth.

Did you enjoy it?

Do you want another one?

Take Two: Genesis 2

Retelling the tale as adventure
Man is in need of a mate
Stuff about rivers
And stuff about trees
A God who just loves to create

God made the first living being
Marrying dust to the breath
Tree an exhibit of
What is prohibited
First feeble shadow of death?

Nothing has worked as companion
Eve enters in from the side
Bone of my bone, also
Flesh of my flesh, the
Attraction cannot be denied.

"Thus will a man leave his father
In one flesh with woman, his equal",
Naked, no shame, and
Happy, no blame, but
A shadow will snake up the sequel.

Look! The Rhythms of Grace

For the Community of St Cuthbert, St Nic's, Durham
Prayer—Hospitality—Study—Justice—Witness

Look up—and pray
Pray for all you're worth
Pray for everyone, and everything
Pray in all things, not knowing how it works
Pray for new life and new birth
Look up and pray

Look around—and welcome
Hospitality of the heart
Making space for neighbours, and for all
Hospitable in all things, not knowing how it happens
That those welcomed come to play their part
Look around and welcome

Look down—and study
Settle your hearts on the sacred pages
Study every chapter, and every verse
Study at all times, not knowing nearly enough
Of the life-giving wisdom of the ages
Look down and study

Look out—for justice
Act justly for all the earth
Love mercy for the needy, and all God's creation
Walk humbly in all things, not knowing where it leads
Justice bringing hope for all to birth
Look out for justice

Look here—it is harvest time
Good news—the *evangel*—be bold!
Good news today and good news for all time
Good news to all people, not knowing how it is
That the seed brings fruit a hundredfold
Look here for harvest

Look—the Lord comes
And delights to lead us on
To joyful abandon
To heart-full abundance
To the rhythms of his grace

Your Kingdom Coming

Commissioning service

You were always
Set in motion as
The envoy to the North
　　To dance and not grow faint, for
　　　　Forgotten sons and daughters.

The Lord's Prayer.
Reluctant. Unmumbled.
So ferry me, across the water,
With my bag clasped to my side
　　Uncoiled foreign accents, for
　　　　Forgotten strangers.

You were always
Deep behind the frontline
Gracing the wastes of the Western world
Breaking the back of the wilderness
Laughing deep into the heartland
　　The traffic breathes
　　With the coming wind
　　The growing rattle and hum
　　　　Go now. Into the world
　　　　And spread abroad your fortune
　　　　To leave no trace but only
　　　　　　Forgotten memories
　　　　　　Always returning.

Summer Mission Team

The distant strain of a far-away train
The sunlight setting on a deserted street
Walking where the frontlines meet
In footsteps of summer rain.

Town square warm in the sudden storm
Hosting faceless painted faces
Preaching the gospel face-to-places
Lonely streets on form.

Waiting on with the crowd all gone
And a trembling heart in an unknown pain
Long after the mind has taken the strain—
Touched in the sundown song.

A half-played hand in the barren land
Leaves restlessness and wonder twinned
Held like a candle in the wind
As love stakes out its stand.

Now, since then—I come alive when
With memories quick to the joyful plunder
The heart erupts in simple wonder
And walks that Earth again.

Three Funeral Visits and a Wedding: Parish Life

Another week in parish
A week of beating bounds
Another week of visits
A week of doing rounds

Eve was always lovely
Ted was always kind
Grace had such a friendly face
Who said love is blind?

Another week of planning
Days of calls and dates
Arranging the rehearsals
Juggling the plates

Ted was never angry
Grace's hug was wide
Eve was sweet as cherry pie
You may kiss the bride

Another morning listening
Tales of love and strife
Shadows of the vale of tears
Loved and leaving life

Grace had wanted children
Ted so loved his dogs
Eve was married in the war
None of them had jobs

Another wide-eyed couple
Can we use an owl?
To fly in carrying the rings
It's all the fashion now

We gather here in sadness
We gather through our loss
The family told me this week that
She "liked to be the boss"

Another "Dear, beloved"
Another "Stand to sing"
Another "Say this after me"
And "Do you have the ring?"

Another week in parish
The joy, the hurt, the real
The celebrating, up and down
The turning of the wheel

Baptized into loving
Brimming full of joy
I now pronounce you man and wife
We celebrate the gift of life
The body silent by the grave
The bouncing baby boy

How We Brought the Good News to Ghent

On the river road from Sas van Gent
Light leaks from refineries
Enormous steel monoliths
That twinkle on the water

    Belief and hope and silent words that
    Drown beneath the rumble of
    Orange industrial nightshift
    Lie floating on the waves

River mist enshrouds the car that
Like a hollow bullet streaks
From station on to station
Blasting headlights to the shore

    Rattle to the rising bridge that
    Yawns into the emptiness
    A ship screams to the seascape
    Echoes, rolling, to the banks

Safe within the heart, sitting
Safe behind the wheel
Beneath this co-creation as it
Slaves on through the night

 There between the darkness
 Lying crystallized in wait is
 The Spirit of the Lord as He
 Hovers on the waters

No springing to the saddle, then
Except a simple confidence in
One who goes before us, as
The good news came to Ghent

Mid-Week Bible Study

Gentle faces, gentle lives
Nervously arrive
Tea and coffee, mid-week study
Bibles at our sides

Gathered round the sacred page our
Different points of view
In our sharing, in our talking
Scripture speaks anew

Reading Ruth or hearing Esther—
God of daily light—
Ancient Israel, modern England
Wintry Wednesday night

Hope for all our burdened living
Riches for the poor
Gentle faces, bolder lives
Heading out the door.

Not of this Worldview

Paris

From the steps of Montmartre
Washed in the twilight
Over painted mirrors reflecting
I look to the sovereign skyline

Pilgrims skid on sanded stairs
To the shadow of the Sacred Heart;
All-night cafés lend their life
To the night of the city of light

Just as the holy relics change
From likeness into likeness,
And light from Dante's postcard stall
Has overcome the darkness,
No candles pray a path to you,
But vision fills the cityscape;
Each neon cypher dancing with
Each sign of God among us.

Covenant

Sleeping heavy in the afternoon
Silence descends like manna
Quakes and eats the sunlight.

A single thin voice says "Know this"

Cuts its way through the darkness
That falls above the carcasses
Still rotting from the day.

There in the blackness
I see a smoking brazier
With blazing torch aflame

It hovers, passes through the pieces.

Impresses then upon me
I am to know for certain . . .
Some rich and textured promise

Of slavery and wretchedness
Of triumph with obedience
Of land for my descendants.

Sins not yet paid for—theirs and mine?

A long life is offered, then
With trouble sure to come.
And this is to be good news.

Or so they will say.

Everyone is Always the First

Everyone is always the first to know
The first to love
The first to grow
Everyone is always the first to have their day

Everyone is always the first to feel
To sense the smell
To taste the real
Everyone is always the first to flex their arm

Everyone is always the first to ache
For love in hand
For mercy's sake
Everyone is always the first to grasp its charm

And everyone is always the last to know
The sacred place
Where spirits flow
Is the stamping ground of all who passed this way

Reading Behind The Lines

Life at theological college (1)—as a student

We believe in mission
We believe in praise, worship, and intercession
We believe in universal suffrage, the rights of the rejected
Practical orthodoxy and political expediency
Radio Free Europe
Calling out from a transit
The voice of the people

We believe in a glorious (though pre-millennial) future
We deconstruct the 1990s
We believe that Barth still speaks through his word today
History contracted to a span
2000 years made incomprehensible

We believe in corporate worship
Let's all stand
In the importance of using the mind
Let's all chant
In understanding what you sing
In your personal response
In "only sing this if it's true for you"
We believe in the *ipsissima vox evangelica*
Calling out from a transit
This is the voice of America
Broadcasting all over the Ancient Near East

We believe in academic Liberation Theology seminars
Putting the church right on evangelism
The glorious history of missions
"God Save The Queen" and
The introduction of *Hymns of Light and Love* to
    the Himalayan foothills
It's been a long long way from foot-washing to foot-noting
(Please do not wash feet in the library)

We believe in the eternal significance of
    the culturally conditioned word
In the endless endurance of non-air-conditioned lectures
In the significance of the symbolism
(Please do not take silver spoons through
    the bathroom window)
We just move now into a time of quiet

. . .

. . .

. . .

We accidentally submitted a note to the milkman
    as an essay on Mesopotamian Flood Myths and
    now have more milk than we can drink
We believe that the parable of the sheep and
    the goats lacks the early, though disputed,
      "When did we see you hungry *after having*
      signed in for lunch and not feed you?"
We believe that a book the size of a
    mustard seed is a real blessing

We believe that now that we at last are here
God is going to be ok. After all
Isn't that how it works?
What could possibly go wrong?

Watching the American Dream Go By

It's not the heat that kills you
It's not the blinding skies
Or the stifling shafts of sunlight
Grinding hope out of your eyes.
It's not the filtered water
Or the dead recycled air
It's not the easy emptiness
The fixed and friendly stare.
It's not the passing freeway
Turning day and night to naught
Or the sudden interruptions
Crowding out the idle thought.
It's not the space that kills you
It's not the room to move
It's not the menu options that
Have nothing left to prove.
It's not the light that kills you
Whiter than the brightest white
Or the gospel choir chorus
In the cafe on your right
It's not the fear of violence
In this city on a hill.
Or the teeth. Or the smile.
Or the promise of a pill.

It's that they could have had it all
They had it there for the taking
They seized the possibility
And lived it in its making
It could have been the Eden
Abandoned since the fall
And instead it's life on earth . . .
"New every morning, after these messages."

It's not the first amendment
It's not the key lime pie
It's not the walking on the moon
The fireworks in July.
It isn't Chappaquiddick
Was never JFK
(Was maybe Agent Orange?)
It wasn't LBJ
It's not consumer freedom
It isn't Britney Spears
It might be Mickey Mouse.
It's not for lack of tears
It can't be in the water
Or area 51
Can it? Is it censored?
It isn't too much sun.
It's not the war on terror
The statue of . . . of . . . who was that
    one with the torch? . . .
It's not the screen door slamming

The mosquitoes on the porch
If nothing's too much trouble then
It's not the forced compliance
It isn't really politics
It isn't rocket science.
It's not the civil liberties
Or basketball or sex
Or skywalks in Atlanta
Or talk-show nervous wrecks
It's not the state of Medicare
Or family therapy
It was briefly Charles Manson
—the Mason-Dixon line; the KKK—
It isn't me.

    All this fruit that looks so good to eat
    To taste, to touch, to have, to hold
    The land's eternal rhythms, from
    Its desert heat to snowbound cold
    Who has the moral high ground?
    Whose shadowlands are pure?
    Who thinks they're any better? . . .
    "With more to come, right after this"

It's not the road less travelled
The Blue Ridges, The Ozarks
It's not the Dallas beltway
Of course not Rosa Parks
It's not the strawberry sundae
It isn't apple pie
Or David Foster Wallace
Hanging limply from the sky.
It couldn't be the IRS,
Was not Enola Gay
Dealing out the end of time.
Is it the NRA?
It's not the new technology
It's not the overweight
Or the scale of Mount Rushmore
Or the money tempting fate.
It's not the Shenandoah
Rolling gloaming to the deep
And not the Mississippi's
Mighty continental creep
It isn't in the farmsteads
And it's barely in the beer
It isn't sold at Christmas
Or upgraded at New Year.
There isn't time to catch it
On the early evening news
It isn't preached by imams
Nor is it in the pews
It's not the fault of atheists

Or communists or Jews
It isn't even broadcast—we believe—
By Fox. It's not your shoes.

It's not despair that kills you
Double latte. Hold the whip.
It's not the maddest Wall Street hour
Or Enron going down the dip.
It's not Alaska's oil fields
The lower forty-eight.
Aloha! Not Hawaii
Nor Elvis '68.
Was it ever Al Capone?
Marlon Brando's padded cheeks?
Reagan's foreign policy?
The festival of weeks?
They say you still hear Hendrix
Playing out the Woodstock crowd.
Remove your shoes and dignity
No liquids are allowed.
It's not the GPS that sends you
Sideways to the lake
It's not the tendency to think
My sin is your mistake.

It's that they caught the glimpse of heaven
The dream that says *"I Am!"*
As they terraformed the wilderness
And built the Hoover Dam
But you cannot build perfection
Or dry up every tear
Or fix the broken hearted . . .
"Who'll be telling us their story after the break."

It's not in San Francisco
It's not the fear of death
It isn't Orson Welles constructing
Rosebud's final breath.
It isn't Scott Fitzgerald
It isn't Maybelline
It wasn't segregation—
Though it really should have been.
You travel through West Texas
And you hear the tolling bell
It isn't calling anyone
To dinner or to hell.
Not waking in the afternoon
And waiting for a word
Not shooting hot-dogs skywards
At the bottom of the third.
It isn't in Montana
Like most things in this life
It wasn't Michael Jackson
It's not the trophy wife.

It isn't kids out giggling
And counting up their toes
It isn't snowstorms, glowing fires
And milk and Oreos.
It isn't life in Leavenworth
Or touring Alcatraz
The Macy's front at Christmas
Or New Orleans jazz.
It wasn't Jimmy Carter
—A man whose time has come?—
Or Mabel waiting table
Raising money for her son.
It isn't in the pay-check
And it isn't in the lot.
It wasn't Vietnam . . . ah
Believe it or not . . .
It isn't Whitman's *Leaves of Grass*
It isn't Stephen Crane
It isn't Henry Fonda
(and it certainly wasn't Jane)
Is it Waco? Is it Catholics?
Is it Marilyn Monroe?
Is it Broadway? Is it Vegas?
Is it ever right to disrupt, cancel or reschedule the show?
Step away from the heartland
Keep your hands above your head.
It's not that crime is up (or down)
Or blue, or maybe red?
It's not a purple dinosaur

It isn't Dr Seuss
It isn't infomercials
Now endorsed for public use.
I wonder if the founding fathers
Saw it come to this?
To Hollywood? To Watergate?
To park'n'ride'n'kiss?
Is it possible it's prayer in schools?
Or preachers preaching hell?
Or the San Andreas fault?
Or the Morrison Hotel?
Perhaps it was the companies
Who sold the cigarettes?
It wasn't Johnny Carson
Or the Packers or the Mets.
It wasn't Halle Berry
—You couldn't understand—
We have our reservations
East and West across the land.
It wasn't at the Alamo
It wasn't Pickett's Charge
It didn't ride with Paul Revere.
It isn't extra-large.
It can't be requisitioned
By the cops, the FBI
It won't be coming home again
From Dunkirk or My Lai.
It isn't on Mulholland and
It may not happen soon

It isn't jailed at Joliet
Or howling at the moon.
It's not in Coronado
Underneath the navy crest
It doesn't shine its shoes today
Or wear its Sunday best.

I think I see it shining
In the fast lane, out of reach
I thought I saw the sickle
Glinting darkly at the beach.
I believe I heard it waiting
Where the Rockies meet the sky.
In the nothingness of everything.
We live. And then we die.

So they could have had it all?
So they held it in their hand?
America. The Eighth Day
The uncreated land?
The eye is on the dollar bill
God rest his soul with thee . . .

And there was evening.
And there was morning.
And there you go, sir.
You have a nice day, now.

Sabbath

Strain

Work to rule

Hard graft. No thanks. Longing

Flailing and Failing

Shudders to a rest

Gift of the Spirit

Sabbath

Pain

Brought to bear

Hard labour. If you want it. Endless

Flying. Trying

Shudders to a death

Gift of the Spirit

Sabbath

Rebirth

Fleet of foot

New eyes. New heart. New law

Waiting. Breathing

Bristles to awareness

Gift of Resurrection

Sabbath

Simple Joy

Heavy rain at night
Sunset in the park
Eating lemon cake
Silence in the dark

Morning by a lake
Coffee any time
Healthy appetite
Slipping into rhyme

Singing ever higher
Baking bread for lunch
Resting on a hill
Winning on a hunch

Visiting the ill
Sharing in delight
Dinner by the fire
Heavy rain at night

Skipping Along to Another Big Story

For Christina/ Seymour/Robyn—at the launch of their
"One Big Story" story-telling project for schoolchildren

Two kids talking. Tell me a story
Life comes crawling, out of the dark
One kid smiling. Seeing opportunity
Lightning striking, catching the spark

Three kids playing. Acting the story
Making a world. Baptizing the sky
One kid laughing. Seeing her opening
Entering a world and daring to try

Four kids drawing. Painting a heaven
Filling the background with joy, delight
Choosing the cast and peopling paradise
Holding a candle, into the night

Five kids caring. Creating and calling
Dancing the moment, shaping the space
One kid beaming. Burning with passion
Brimming with beauty, flooding her face

Six kids acting. Shouting and silencing
Stage right—stage left. Upright and bold
One kid thinking. Imagining differently
Pulling in shy ones out from the cold

Seven kids celebrating. Finished. Perfected
Ringed and rejoicing. Jabbering aloud
Proud of creating, dreaming of futures
Empowered. Amazed. Awestruck. Wowed

One kid happy. Falling to sleep again
One world lightened. One heart clever
One pair of eyes sees whole new frequencies
One life changed. One person. Forever.

Eternal City

Summer in Rome
Hotter yet still hotter
They call it "the inferno" (in fact, that year, "the Lucifer")
Fountains in the streets
Bring some relief

The Colosseum
The Roman Forum
Palatine Hill resplendent
Ice cream—gelato
Cools us, a little

The Vatican!
. . .
Michelangelo
. . .
Astonishing

We take the bus
Down the Appian Way
And discover the catacombs
Step into history
Finally
Cool
As back
In time we go
And discover true eternity
In the Eternal City

Heat meets dark
Death meets life
Earth meets sky
Hope wins

And to Think That We Saw
It in Vatican Square

Now the first thing we saw in Vatican Square
Is that the square is a circle
Don't ask me why
And a large gathering of nuns from the American Midwest
Was just passing by

Well the second thing we saw in Vatican Square
Was security check-in barriers if you want to see the Pope
—and sadly, you can see why.
A Brazilian volleyball-playing youth group
And a large gathering of nuns from the American Midwest
Were just passing by.

Then the third thing we saw in Vatican Square
Was the ring of Bernini's famous statues
Set against the sky.
Two Polish backpackers, an Australian family on tour,
A Brazilian volleyball-playing youth group
And a large gathering of nuns from the American Midwest
Were just passing by.

The next thing we saw—and heard—in Vatican Square
Was a boys' choir from Rwanda
Whose song rose on high.
A German table-tennis team, a party of Mormon tourists,
Two Polish backpackers, an Australian family on tour,
A Brazilian volleyball-playing youth group
And a large gathering of nuns from the American Midwest
Were just passing by.

It seemed that all of life was there.
Someone said that a "group" of nuns is a "superfluity",
While a young Portuguese couple did juggling tricks
And an Austrian church on pilgrimage
From the St Francis Way laughed without a care.
As a German table-tennis team, a
     party of Mormon tourists,
Two Polish backpackers, an Australian family on tour,
A Brazilian volleyball-playing youth group
And the nuns from the American Midwest
All gathered in Vatican Square.

Malaysian toddlers ran in and out of the colonnades
Priests took turns framing photos against the obelisk
A Scottish minister shuffled uncomfortably
 in the heat with his family
Four Canadian teenagers were
 disappointed to discover that
The Hard Rock Cafe just down the street
Was not selling Vatican City Hard Rock T-shirts
Eight young French women in
 wheelchairs sang as they were
Pushed by their guardian Cistercian monks
An excited Korean couple bought a rosary
And an Englishman tried to write it all down
While the gelato stand just off sacred soil
Offered sweet cooling delight to . . .
A German table-tennis team, a party of Mormon tourists,
Two Polish backpackers, an Australian family on tour,
A Brazilian volleyball-playing youth group
And a large gathering of nuns from the American Midwest
Awaiting a blessing, or simply enjoying the chance
To say that they were there.

And to think that we saw it in Vatican Square.

Sunset in Tuscany

The sun sets in Tuscany
The cicadas start up
The peace is full of noise
The noise is full of peace

The longest part of day
Is evening's graceful sweep
The dark is full of light
The day has found release

The soul comes out at night
The heart breathes again
The world is full of space
The generous "Amen"

The noise is full of light

The dark is full of peace

The Reader and the Wall

Slow he lowers himself into position
Hunched, haunched, quiet, still
Lifts his face, lifts his eyes
Begins the crawl across the page
And back
And again across the page
Again back
Line by line by careful line
Breath by breath by stroke by stroke
Steady rhythm, length by length—
Not quickening his oar—
He sets his sights on some far horizon
And crawls again, from left to right,
Steady, steady, steady.

It was not always this way
This graceful glide across the lake
Of text, its surface shimmering
From left to right
And left to right
And always staying steady.
Time was he would have raced ahead
Toward incomprehension
Digesting on some further shore
And towelling himself off, to remove
The trace of line by line by word—
To emerge, triumphant, ruddy-cheeked

Abstracted. Done. And dusted.
But not with water and the word.

That grinding dry engagement
Chafed and blistered: hands, feet, eyes
And he would compensate and rub in all medicament
Unnaturally oiled, fortified by supplements
That went by alien names:
To run and not grow weary
Line by page by book by theme
No water on his back, or
Leaving no mark where he had read
No trace of inward digestion
Till the inside fell away from the outside.
And then one day, or it may have been
One year, or perhaps it was
One time, of unremembered length
He had thought he had seen—sudden
And at the last minute—coming at him
From some unfamiliar angle
The indigestible text, the incommensurate word
The immovable literary object.
Pressed forward, hand outstretched, within
    sight of closing another book
The wall
Beyond which he could not pass
From which he could not draw back
Collision with which he could not avoid.
And stopped.

So now
Undrugged, and unprotected from real encounter
He steps up slowly to the start
And glides in deep, eyes wide open
Long slow breaths, pulling hard
And slow, slow, slow
Line by line
By glorious line
No towel to hand, and never dry
To his own timing
But patient, waiting
Steady rhythm, length by length—
And crawls again, from left to right
Steady, steady, steady.

One day older
A reader at the last

Old and Not Yet Old

The old man is wise, the young man is smart
The young woman cares, the old has a heart

The old saying's sure, the new word is stunning
The new phone is flashy, the old keeps on running

The old coat still fits, the new is in fashion
The new leader's quick, the old one has passion

The old way is grace, the new is ambition
The new version sells, the old has conviction

The old man is slow, the young man is faster—
Both speed and slowness can lead to disaster

The Old Testament is all grace amid sinning
And so is the New, just like the beginning

The old know a truth that will always unfold:
The new and the young have yet to grow old.

Literally

Does "incredible"
Mean "cannot be trusted"?
"Unbelievable"
Mean "cannot be believed"?
When did words slip and
Break from their binding?
It's literally impossible
What cannot be achieved.

Who pays the price when
Words can do anything?
Who counts the cost when
Speech comes cheap?
Who lends promises and
Buys short on rhetoric?
Who is literally asleep?

Who had training for
Unconscious bias?
Or was it subconscious?
Or was I out cold?
It's literally incredible
The stories we are told

All metaphors are
As equal as each other
But some metaphors
Are literally obtuse
Or acute, perhaps?

Does "insane" mean
Wonderfully excessive?
Is it literally mad when
Passive is aggressive?

Whose "free speech" is
Protected by refusing it?
It's literally confusing . . .

Does "open-minded" mean
Literally open to anything?

Is this literally the end of history?

. . .

The Greatest Bookshop in the World

The greatest bookshop in the world—
Northumberland's own Barter Books,
Once a railway terminus in
Alnwick, now a lair that hooks
Enchanted readers, unawares,
Drawn by their imagination,
Jumbled shelves of loved and older
Books, unwinding through the station.

Books for barter, brought in bags by
Readers with a great obsession
Hunting for the perfect book yet
Sitting light to book-possession,
Plus the children's room is joyful;
Model trains run round and zoom
Over bookstacks, while the café
Fills the ancient Waiting Room.

Keep an eye out for the slogan—
Calm and steady, browsing slow
And
Carry baskets overflowing,
On to treasures new we go.

Help yourself to fresh-brewed coffee
Stoke the fire, all the while
Browsing for a book you didn't
Know was there but brings a smile.
Novels, poems, local, foreign,
Rarer books in cabinets
All are welcome, even dogs who
Prowl among the shelves on pets.

Time stands still as lost in wonder
Readers stumble over truth
In communion with the ages
Books convey eternal youth
All of life between two covers
Room by stack by shelf by . . . train
Magical, enchanted space this
Bibliophilic wild terrain.

Online buyers click away to
Doomsday, growing ever manic.
While
The greatest bookshop in the world
Is Barter Books, in northern Alnwick.

*Barter Books, in Alnwick, Northumberland, exists in the
splendour of the converted Victorian building that was once
Alnwick Railway Station (closed 1968). The bookshop opened
in 1991 and operates a barter system offering store credit
for donated books. See <https://www.barterbooks.co.uk/>*

The Ordered Life

The formal ordering
Words on a page
Steps in an age
Poem of life

The fateful beginning
Trail to blaze
Cradle to grave
Stages of life

The fitful believing
Thoughts of a world
Troubled and hurled
Meaning of life

The fearful appearing
Lights in the sky
Heralds on high
Saviour of life

The final accounting
Echoes of good
Grace understood
Story of life

St Catherine's House

Formerly the Mission Church of St Catherine of Alexandria, in the parish of Bearpark, County Durham

The home in which I live was once a church
Whose walls have seen the faithful saints at prayer
And echoed to the praise that filled this air
With thankfulness to God. In my research
St Catherine proved elusive in extreme:
Fourth century, if facts the myths conceal.
Who died upon the breaking Catherine Wheel?
What legend lives on here? Or does it seem
More pressing that the story works its power?
And calls to mind the faithfulness of old
To summon lives of witness to be bold
And rise again in praise. The old bell tower
Still stands, looks down upon me from above,
And God still watches with eternal love.

You've Got a Friend who's not in California

For RR

Most of my Californian friends
Are not in California
They smile and moan about the weather
Will it not get warm here?
Language slides in SoCal asides
Experiences form ya.

Northern Californian friends
Relax and smell the coffee
They see themselves as less laid back
But hey—let's eat banoffee
"It'll be okay, in every way . . ."
Wait . . . no ice in the coffee?

Best way to admire a culture
Isn't from the news
Underneath the broad-brush strokes
People come in ones and twos:
Get to know me, and bestow me
Friendship I won't want to lose.

First Class Second Class

Life at theological college (2)—as a teacher

Can I love you?

Bring me your all
You young, you old
You gleaming bright and bold with big ideas
So confident, so nervous, so shiny with the light
A thousand shards of wrong and right
Ready to interpret
And ready to know
To be lifted up
To be brought down low
To essay a thought into a line
To smile, to frown, to cry, to slow . . .
To see how vast the land must be
And then, again,
To pray

And can I still love you?

Back again this year
Older, wiser, better grasping
Just how far there is to go
And just how far we've come.
More questions
Could you say that again?

But what about the verse that says . . .
"On what I can and can't accept"
On learning to live with
Those with whom we disagree
On almost everything, but not quite.
Still holding fast to roots and convictions
So quiet, so calm, learning to behold
Truth with peace.

Do I, in fact, love you?

First year class
Second year class
Some more equal than others
Weeping with those who weep
Rejoicing with those who rejoice
Often on the same day
Shepherd of the sheep
Always out of my depth
But always knowing that the question remains:

Can I love you again today?

The Song After the Night Before

*"In every generation one is obligated to see oneself
as one who personally went out from Egypt."*
Mishnah: Pesachim 10.5

(i) Genesis 3

One day out of Eden
All is not lost
We still have each other
Though Adam seems distracted
Asks who brought the fruit? And what are these skins for?
And is work, seriously, what it is going to be about?
He thinks *he* has problems, I say, *sotto voce*

(ii) Exodus 15

One day out of Egypt
All is not lost
No really—we have so much to be thankful for!
Sorry, I can't hear myself think
With the song of the sea
And the roaring of the sea
And the nothing ever going to be the same again

(iii) Exodus 33

One day after the golden calf
All is not lost . . . I think
There was a lot of talking at the front of the camp
Moses was angry. God was angry. It is
   hard to tell the difference
Confident men say we learn from our mistakes
And will never do that again.
The wise are saying nothing.

(iv) 1 Samuel 21

One day out in the wilderness with David
All is not lost
We fly by night
We take food where we find it
Though whether showbread is fair game
   causes some dispute
And we circle endlessly around Saul, the Lord's anointed
Wondering where the anointing will land

(v) 1 Kings 12

One day after the split
All is not lost
Though these new border checkpoints
Were a thing that should not have been in Israel
Or Judah, or whatever we are going to call it now
And there are a lot of broken hearts on the ground
Not that you would know that from the politicians

(vi) 2 Kings 25

One day out of Jerusalem
—Ach!—
All is lost

(vii) Ezra-Nehemiah

We read the law
We build the walls
Life goes on
Never the same again, again?

Love

Love is when I—when you're gone—I
Realize all I haven't said. When
All the earth is mine alone, and
All of space is in my bed.

If . . .
Love is joy with happy thoughts, I
Realize all I could have said. If
Setting forth the least of these, would
Turn the light on in my head.

Love exhumes the heart of darkness
And exhausts the swell of dread. I
Journey far and still confess that
There is too much left unsaid.

So . . .
Love is one and all to me, and
Love to you a path I tread. If
Love gives flight to all that's free, I
Choose to rest with you instead:

To rest, to run, to not grow weary
Led on high. Rejoicing. Wed.

To Keith Green

Keith Green (1953–82), gospel
singer, died in a plane crash

Evening shadows stalk me
So high above the clouds
Where once did Buddy Holly
Take three short steps to heaven

Someone moved the goalposts
Someone called you home
Where Manchester United
Left Munich for the skies . . .

Someone shot John Lennon
He never left the ground
Someone walked on water
You followed in his footsteps

You couldn't wait to get there
You had no round trip ticket
But what would you have taken
If the booking desk had asked?

Did you want to go back to Texas?
Did that ever cross your mind?
Or had you seen the angels?
Beheld the son of man?

Were there any last regrets?
Relationships left broken?
I somehow can't imagine that
You left too much unsaid

Now the music haunts me—
Creates in me a clean heart
And if this plane should never land . . .
Will you do requests?

The John the Baptist Files

(1) John the Baptist sets out his Manifesto

I am John the Baptist
The kingdom is at hand
I've come to tell you that you must repent.
I've seen the darkest corners
Of our lives and of our hearts and now
I've cried for you and now you must repent.
The axe is at the root
Of the multi-purpose tree—
Part symbol of our lives
And of our times—
My heart has wept for you
And I offer life to you
But I have to tell you that
You must repent.

Do this now
To fulfil all righteousness.

(2) John the Baptist Arrives for a Speaking Tour of England

I am John the Baptist
With something to declare
I have no luggage—just the camel hair
In which I stand here
Yes really
I can do no other.

Nature of visit?
A few speaking engagements.
Length of stay?
A mission week or two.
Intent to cause trouble while on British soil?
Not at all.
I intend only to serve the one
On whom the ends of the ages has come.

They wave me through.

(3) John the Baptist is Guest Preacher at the Cathedral

I am John the Baptist
Thank you Revd Higgins
I'm delighted to be here
And to all the Dean and Chapter
Thank you
And such moving music from the choir
Thank you all
For those who do not know me
I am John the Baptist

Our text today is from the prophets
—You cannot beat the prophets
You can run them out of town
But you cannot keep them down
And as we turn to the prophets
You know, in a strange sort of way, I am reminded
Of another turning, a turning of the heart and mind
And where I come from we have a word for that
Which translated is "repent" . . .
And as I was on my way here today . . .

Civil religion?
Strange times.

(4) John the Baptist Speaks at New Life Blessing Church of Joy

I am John the Baptist
Repent!
Turn the ship around!
Prepare to meet thy maker!
You never know, when you walk out of here tonight . . .
Come on down
Hallelujah!
Hearts and souls
"Just as I am"!

Greatest hits.
They loved it.

(5) John the Baptist is No-Platformed by the Student Union and Puts Out a Statement

I am John the Baptist
Let me set the record straight
It's always been quite clear what I believe.
With no false intent did I
Accept the invitation to
Address the Christian Union mission week.
I never once intended
To address the matters raised
In this travesty of full and frank debate—
None of these were on my mind:
Not race, and never gender,
Nor self-identifications
With which I was not familiar
And I have no real desire
To be dragged into debate
Since all I have to say to you is this:
Repent.
I want to say the kingdom
Awaits in expectation
Judgment is at hand and yet
All of this is good for us.

Good news?!
They did not believe me

(6) John the Baptist is Speaker
at the Mothers' Union

I am John the Baptist
I don't want any cake.
It's kind of you to have me
But I don't want any cake.
Do I have some slides from Israel?
And pictures of my journey?
Well I—
And is it true I eat locusts?
No, just the berries, but—
And would I like some tea?
Good people, listen . . .
. . . I have something to say.

We must turn our lives around and live for God.

You knew?
You already knew?
You faithful friends
You pilgrim saints
You steadfast souls who have already
Signed up for the long game
Through thick and thin
In joy, in tears, in hope.

Maybe a small slice of honey cake.

(7) John the Baptist Reflects at the End of his Visit to England

Already here among us
And yet still at hand
The kingdom coming.

I need eyes to see
A heart so full of wanting
Needing ears to hear

Still my beating hope
God does not let go.
We are not of this worldview.

My Life as the Search for the Perfect Book

It started long ago with
Snow! by Dr Seuss
It had to be the best!
The best ever!
Though was not the funniest
That was *The Puffin Joke Book*
Which wore thin on the ears of my family
Who were doubtless pleased
When I hid myself away to devour
Dr Who and the Planet of the Daleks
Over a hundred pages of unputdownable action
Undetained by character development.
The NME Encyclopaedia of Rock'n'Roll
Became a trusted friend through teenage years
And then I discovered, one day, out of the blue
Rosencrantz and Guildenstern are Dead
And all my understanding of language
Was stopp'd, as it were. So then,
The life of a playwright for me. Though
While I waited for that to unfold
I went hitch-hiking through Douglas Adams'
Dirk Gently's Holistic Detective Agency
Which was—in its awkwardly strange way—
All about me, as I went to a college a little
Like the one in the book. Though
Not much like it, on reflection.

Wittgenstein's *Philosophical Investigations*
Was left conspicuously beside the bed
In my student room, until a friend
Who actually had read a book or two
Pointed me to literature—
Vast untrodden and unsuspected field
Who gets to play here? To live and work here?
What Maisie Knew and *Heart of Darkness*
T. S. Eliot, like every student before or since,
War and Peace (though in due time I would find
The French Manga version more comprehensible,
no, really)
And also *The British Museum is Falling Down*
Which was certainly about me,
Though again, not that much, on reflection.

These latter years have been as full of candidates
As all my book-filled former years had been.
Jonathan Strange and Mr Norrell was magic, while
Black Swan Green actually was about me, really.
Clive James spun webs around the world
With *Cultural Amnesia*. And then
I finally tackled *Infinite Jest*, and was won over by,
And hopelessly lost within,
The world according to David Foster Wallace,
At last finding a book that was not about me
But that spoke in tune—though not in harmony—
With all manner of musing
In my mind's eye.

Meanwhile . . .

Along had come children
And reading at bedtime stopped being
The long, slow trek through *The Corrections*
And became instead the collected adventures of
Preston Pig. Or indeed, to complete the tale,
Of Dr Seuss, asking always
"I want to know—do you like snow?"
Again! Again!
Giggle, wriggle
Snuggle under covers
Turn out the light.

Good night.

Unexpected Interviews with Holy Men

I missed my real calling as a rock star
And drifted into teaching in the East
Had eleven years of doing TESOL
Headed home and trained to be a priest.

—

I used to be a lawyer down in London
And worked for trafficked victims in my time
Now I run a church plant, inner-city
And am grateful for experience of crime.

—

Twenty-seven years I was a doctor
Bandaging the hurt in A&E
I wanted to do more than heal the body
Though now it's hard to see the enemy.

—

Stories flow on deep and rich and thicker—
"What the vicar did" before being vicar.

Return Visit

Turbulence like birth pains
Descending from the sky
We're being reborn.
Someone, somewhere
Has made straight a runway
Preparing for our coming.
You're staring at me
Blank, uncomprehending,
I'm remembering . . . we used to be
Such good friends.
Separated now only by customs
But I'm wanting to learn
All about you (again).

Pharaoh Ponders Brexit

Moses came to see me saying "Let my people go"
I can't imagine such a people exit
They worship a strange God who my
    advisors do not know

And somehow they all want to vote for Brexit.
"Unity is strength" and other slogans that I use
To keep the workforce happy in their toil
But Moses and his brother aren't that easy to confuse
The issue seems to turn on foreign soil.

They'll miss the many blessings that
    Egyptian union brings
I find their manifesto rather vague
It focuses on symbols and on patriotic things
Not sure that it would help them in a plague . . .

And Moses Replies:

Pharaoh doesn't get that it is not about the state
Though his failure to do justice is endemic
It's worship of the one true God of Israel that's at stake
Not politics or pride or a pandemic.

So hear this well Pharaoh
God says "Let my people go".
That's all you know on earth
Or need to know.

A Light Psalm

Ready to press "go"
  On the copying machine:
A burning shining light moves
  Across my field of vision
It knows my page completely
  Recreates it in its image
And leaves me with a copy
  Indelible and perfect.

Daily I awake, Lord
  And you are pressing "go"
As a burning shining light moves
  Between the two horizons
—Past, present, future lie
  Illumined in your gaze
A headlight on my car
  And a streetlight on my way.

You are the backlit tablet
    The laptop saving energy
Your flashing cursor guides me
    Through my day—across your page
And Lord you pull the plug
    On the screens of the unscrupulous:
A bug in all their programs
    As their power dies away.

So shine, Lord, shine
    Eternal power generator
Light on my Christmas tree
    Candle at my mass.
Keep me till your dawning and
    Between your two horizons
Be the headlight on my car
    And a streetlight on my way.

Assistant Worship Leader Seeks Meaningful Relationship

Lover

I read the books on purity and passion
I sing the soaring solo every Sunday
I pray in muttered tongues up on the platform
I stack the shelves at Tesco's every Monday

With one hand in the air
I can strike the perfect pose
But will I find the perfect match?
Heaven knows.

"Assistant worship leader
Seeks meaningful relationship
Must be a singer and a
Calvinist preferred
Likes to travel overseas and
Likes to meet new faces
And loves to spend time
In the Word."

Beloved

Lord I believe in the power of praise
I bless the one who raises up the meek
I balance poise and passion in the chorus
I stack the shelves at Tesco's every week

    With lips that kiss the microphone
    I strike the perfect pose
    But will I find the one for me?
    Heaven knows.

        "Assistant worship leader
        Seeks meaningful relationship
        Somebody to share with on
        The bad days and the good
        Knows *The Seven Keys to*
        A Deeper Walk With Jesus
        Would like to find someone
        Who understood."

Slow

Instant life
Take this step
Get on board!

Instant wisdom
Read this book
Get wise!

Instant virtue
Pray this prayer
Get good!

Instant justification
Claim this gift
Get right!

Instant joy
Sing this song
Get happy!

Instant perseverance
—Slow down
Could take a while

Memories

Carry me back
>   To innocent memories
>   Of days in painted sunshine
>   You were laughing by the well
>   By the deep deep waters
>   And you sang to fill the skies
Well that takes me back
>   To London city nightlife
>   Gargoyled Leicester Square
>   Crowds at turning out time
>   With doorways selling sanctuary
>   That have nothing on
A single homespun memory
>   Of hair blowing lightly in the wind
>   Along the lines of melody
>   That carried to the treetops
>   The fulness of your joy.
>   Considering the lilies
That really takes me back.

Raffle Winners

I messed up my diary
(Re-)discovering Thursday night's church meeting
On Monday, when I was actually
At a conference in LA

Flew Wednesday night
Arriving home disorientated but happy
In time to eat quickly before
Driving to church.

Five thousand miles
To arrive in the middle of a friendly argument
About where to put raffle winners' names
On the notice board.

Different perspectives.
It's hard to have an opinion over such long distances
Maybe things always depend on
Where you are coming from?

Compassion

The gift of tears
Washes clear
The eyes of the heart

Now clear-sighted
Bitter-sweet
Weep with those who weep

Yet still free
To rejoice
With those who rejoice

Turn again to
Comfort and
Mourn with those who mourn

Find no words to
Yet compare
Fragile gift of tears

The Promise of Life: Four Vows and a Funeral

Born and baptized
I knew nothing about it
It marked me for life
I would not be without it

Married and joined
In covenant loving
Marks me for joy
Trusted and trusting

Later confirmed
Kneeling for blessing
Marking me out as a
Pilgrim confessing

Called and ordained
Deacon and priest
Marks me for service
Burdens released

These are the days
When "yes" has been "yes"
Marking me ready for
God's faithfulness

One more to come
The promised "Amen"
Marked out in death
For new life again

"Why Are You Wanting Jimmy Baptized?"

The curate sits nervously asking the question
"Why are you wanting your Jimmy baptized?"
The father is puzzled and looks to the mother
The mother is cooing, avoiding their eyes

"My Gran would have wished it—it's just what we do"
She bounces young Jimmy on each of her knees
"We've got thirteen cousins and seventeen aunties
And Millie who'd like to play violin please"

The curate is sweating and starting to wonder
If baptism visits will ever go well
When Dad says "The reason we're wantin' 'im done is
To make sure that Jimmy will not go to hell".

The curate thinks back to theology classes
And struggles to frame an appropriate line
But Jimmy is fussing, the doorbell is ringing
And all he can say is "I'm sure that it's fine".

"Is that it?" the Mum asks while taking a phone call
"Is everything good? Can our Jimmy get done?"
And lo and behold by next Sunday they're beaming
And thank the good Lord for the gift of a son.

So then, just one question:
Which way up is God's kingdom really?

In Two Minds

The inquiring mind
Digs deep to find
Questions within questions
And more questions behind

And given time
That way wisdom lies

The acquiring mind
Will tend to bind
Itself within knowledge
But to wisdom is blind

And right away
That is very clever

According to their kinds—
Learning in two minds

Writing a Sermon

Starting from the Bible
Reaching to today
Reeling from the difference
Trying to link a way

Use a funny story
Hang it on a joke—
Scrap the illustration
Sensing it mis-spoke

Try alliteration
Try a one-two-three
"A hope that waits!
A heart that mates!
. . . A style that grates."
Not three points for me

Read another commentary
Try a different tack
Cast a major challenge
Quickly take it back

Talk of something easier
Simpler to explain—
Ruefully return to where
The passage takes the strain

Battling the deadline
Reading in the strife
Suddenly make contact
Spy the word of life

Breaking through the darkness
Springing from the pages
Scrabbling to write it down
Wisdom of the ages

Challenge bringing promise
Gospel bringing grace
Hope reshaping burdens
God is in this place

One more week of living
One more sermon then
One more turning of the page
And we start again.

Hearing a Sermon

Generally getting the point here
Nodding along I agree
Register shift
Losing the drift
Links that I cannot quite see

Loving the story of cycling
Thinking of times when we biked
Couldn't remember
If it was November
Or was that the time when we hiked?

Little bit lost in the passage
Is it God's angry with me?
What did I do?
That last point is true
I hope it was third point of three

It's a bit like the prodigal son
My favourite one of the lot
"When hurting forgive it"
"God loves us—let's live it"
I think that's the gist of the plot

Anyway . . .

Thank you for preaching today!
You certainly make us all think!
I like how you speak
(Who is it next week?)
There are times when I don't get the link

And then times when I do
When the gospel breaks through
And the word of life spinning
Brings joy, so . . . thank you.

Prayer Walk at Barney

*"Barney" is a local name for Barnard
Castle, County Durham*

Not quite the labyrinth
In Chartres Cathedral
Nor for that matter the
Heat of French summer
But patiently walking
The woods above Barney
Seeking to listen to
God in the calm.

Came here to celebrate
God in the everyday
Seeking to hear from him
Fresh once again,
Ministry fading with
Second-hand energy
Needed recharging and
Setting alight.

God of creation and
Maker of pilgrimage
Calling me onward to
Find the right path.
Peaceful and pondering
Prayerful and wandering
Eyes and ears peeled for the
Word from beyond.

Many miles later I
Recognize thankfully
Rhythms of grace have been
Keeping me company—
"*This* is my world, behold
These are my people, and
Here is the way for you,
Go walk in it".

Meeting accomplished and
Weary bones happy I
Turn to the future in
Hope and at peace.

The Valley of the Shadow

Breathe deeply
In the valley of the shadow of death
We could be here a while
In the valley of the shadow of death

Learn to find life in the journey
In the valley of the shadow of death
Learn to see hope all around you
In the valley of the shadow of death

No word is ever the last word
In the valley of the shadow of death
Not even the last word you speak
In the valley of the shadow of death

Kindness breaks the darkness
In the valley of the shadow of death
There is always life to come
In this world or the next
In the valley of the shadow of death

The last enemy will be defeated
In the valley of the shadow of death
Gone before us
The one whose body is no longer here
Saw this place, and chose not to stay
In the valley of the shadow of death
And now waits ahead of us
Calling us onward

Portrait of the Zealot as an Old Man: An Autobiography

Happy in my childhood
Peaceful when a teen
The long slow arc of a very British life
Was rudely interrupted at the age of nineteen

The road to Damascus
Was Uni for me
The blinding light of a sudden conversion
Birthed into certainty, sure as can be

Now I knew everything
Didn't I know it
The sudden zeal of a very fresh convert
Prophet and preacher, but not yet a poet

Jesus didn't come back
That year or the next
The gentler speeds of a long-distance life
Learning to slow down and ponder the text

It's strange now to recall
Cries for revival
The shallow depths of a prayer-light faith
The zeal for a largely unread Bible

Somewhere in my thirties
God called in his debts
The longer reach of a grace-filled nature
Catching me up in the kindest of nets

I wish I could say that
I took to the climb
The rising path of a long walk to freedom
Took time, takes time, will always take time

Slowly and yet surely
Learning all about
The growing grasp of a God of compassion
The candle flickers but never goes out

Learning to be grateful
Even for the zeal
The gain and loss of a life of hindsight:
Accept the turning of the wheel

I would not be here now
Without the kick-start
The precious gift of a transformed life
The abiding love that captures the heart

And I am not there now
Where it all began
The storied life of a faithful learner
Confession of a zealot as an older man

Acknowledgements

I am indebted to the wonderful people at Sacristy Press, especially Natalie Watson, my editor, for the chance to bring together this collection of poems. It has had the longest gestation of anything I have written. It truly blossomed in the past year when Richard Rohlfing Jr prodded and prompted me to take up poetry again as I was recovering from illness. Thank you, Richard, for your encouragement, and for getting me involved in an excellent conference entitled *New Song: Biblical Hebrew Poetry as Jewish and Christian Scripture for the 21st Century* at Durham's Ushaw College in the summer of 2019, in the proceedings of which a version of the poem "The Song After the Night Before" will be published. Three other poems included here were first published in different versions in a book of short stories I once wrote: *It's Been a Quiet Week in the Global Village* (London: SPCK/Triangle, 1999).

Heartfelt thanks to Melody Briggs, for love and support always, and for being a first reader of extraordinary grace; and to our three unexpectedly poetic children – Josh whose first prize in a creative writing contest when he was aged ten probably means he has still earned more from creative writing than I have; Kristin for the stunning image on the front cover and introducing me to villanelles; and Matthew who has himself already written and published poetry more than once. I am thankful to my sister Patricia for her lifelong friendship, including sharing a love of literature—it is a great pleasure to dedicate this book to her.

Lightning Source UK Ltd.
Milton Keynes UK
UKHW011827080321
380007UK00001B/90